MINECRAFT

SCIENCE & ENVIRONMENT
OFFICIAL WORKBOOK

CO_2

TOM BOLTON

INTRODUCTION

HOW TO USE THIS BOOK

Welcome to an exciting educational experience! Your child will go on a series of adventures through the enchanting world of Minecraft, practising Science, Technology, Engineering and Mathematics (STEM) skills along the way. Including content matched to the National Curriculum for science for ages 7–11, this workbook takes your child into fascinating landscapes where our heroes Cam and Leela embark on building projects and scientific journeys of discovery.

As each adventure unfolds, your child will complete topic-based questions worth a certain number of emeralds. Answers are included at the back of the book and the emeralds earned can be 'traded in' on the final page.

At the end of each chapter, your child will have the opportunity to complete projects in Minecraft itself, applying the educational knowledge that has been learned in hands-on, science-inspired tasks. Each chapter concludes with a short project notebook where your child can reflect on their achievements.

MEET OUR HEROES

Cam has a big personality! He likes the sights and sounds of exciting new things, but doesn't always take the time to delve deeper. He loves animals, especially scary ones like polar bears and wolves. He is excited about science but sometimes jumps to conclusions without checking facts.

Cam has a naturally artistic eye and uses inspiration from the world around him. He likes precious ores, such as diamond and emerald, but doesn't always see the appeal of plants and rocks. Cam enjoys looking for treasure chests and using redstone to launch fireworks.

Leela is a thinker. She finds fascination in the small details that are not always obvious at first glance. She thinks rocks are intriguing as they tell us about the past; and she loves plants because they are so adaptable and complex.

Leela is knowledgeable about science and always checks facts to make sure she understands correctly. She has a natural concern for the environment and always sees the connections across different subjects. She enjoys archaeology, potion brewing and classifying organisms.

CONTENTS

First published In 2024 by Collins
An imprint of HarperCollins*Publishers*
1 London Bridge Street, London, SE1 9GF

HarperCollins*Publishers*
Macken House, 39/40 Mayor Street Upper,
Dublin 1, D01 C9W8, Ireland

All images are © 2024 Mojang AB,
© Shutterstock.com or © HarperCollins*Publishers*

Publishers: Jennifer Hall and Fiona McGlade
Author: Tom Bolton
Project management: Richard Toms
Design and typesetting: Ian Wrigley
Cover: Sarah Duxbury
Production: Bethany Brohm

Special thanks to Kelsey Ranallo, Jay Castello, Alex Wiltshire,
Sherin Kwan and Milo Bengtsson at Mojang, and the team
at Farshore

ISBN: 978-0-00-865423-8

British Library Cataloguing in Publication Data.

A CIP record of this book is available from the
British Library.

1 2 3 4 5 6 7 8 9 10

Printed in India by Multivista Global Pvt.Ltd.

PREPARE FOR YOUR ADVENTURE

PROJECT BUILDS

The project builds at the end of each chapter are science-inspired challenges that you can complete yourself in Minecraft. You can tackle these challenges by creating a new world each time, or you can complete all project builds in a single Minecraft world.

To complete all six chapters in the same world, it is important that you write down the coordinates of the different biomes you travel to. You can then use the **teleport command** to travel to each biome when you want to carry on your scientific work in that area.

You can write down the coordinates of your build locations in the table below.

Chapter	Biome / Structure	Coordinates
Life Cycles: Deep in the Mangroves	mangrove swamp	
	beach	
	bamboo jungle	
Plants: Frozen Frontier	ice plains	
Ecosystems: Corals in Crisis	warm ocean	
Rocks: A View to the Past	stony peaks	
Renewable Energy: Fossil Fuels Fiasco	village	
Habitat and Adaptation: Aquatic Enigma	lush caves	

Each project will let you know whether it should be completed in **Creative** or **Survival** mode.

For all projects, you will need to make sure **Cheats** are turned ON and **Show Coordinates** are turned ON in the game settings.

USING THE LOCATE AND TELEPORT COMMANDS

Use the **locate biome** command to find the correct biome for the project builds in each chapter.

For the first chapter, you must locate a **mangrove swamp** biome:

1. Type the following command into the chat:

```
/locate biome mangrove_swamp
```

2. The coordinates of the nearest mangrove swamp will appear on the screen. Write them down.

```
The nearest mangrove_swamp is at block
-1645, 63, 4334 (4227 blocks away)
```

3. Now you can teleport to those coordinates using the **teleport command** (**/tp**) in the chat. Notice that no commas are used in the teleport command.

```
/tp -1645 63 4334
```

4. Hey presto! You are now in a mangrove swamp biome, ready to do your scientific research.

BUILDING A COMMAND CENTRE

If you are a more advanced adventurer, you can create a command centre from where you can teleport to each biome at the push of a button. Make sure you write down the coordinates of your command centre, so you know how to get home!

1. Give yourself a command block by typing the following command into the chat:

```
/give @s command_block
```

2. Place the command block on the ground, with a button just in front of it.

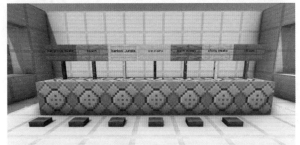

3. Press the use button on the command block. In the Command Input, write the teleport command (tp), the target (@p) and the coordinates of the particular biome.

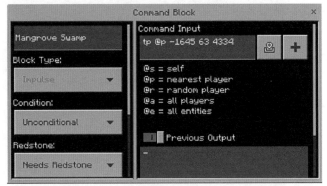

4. At each of your project build locations, it is recommended that you place a command block to teleport you back home to the command centre.

THE CALL TO ADVENTURE

HOME ALONE

When Leela returns home with her friend Cam, she discovers that her father is gone. His important work as a highly skilled potion brewer means he is often away searching for rare ingredients across the Overworld, as well as the realms beyond. His note says he'll be gone for at least a week.

STUCK IN THE VILLAGE

Leela and Cam dream of such urgent and exciting adventures. But most of their days are spent hanging around in the hills surrounding their village of Avondale and exploring the odd, abandoned mineshaft or natural cave system. Leela's father says she's too young to venture beyond the forest.

A LIFE WELL LIVED

The restless pair stare at the item frames on the wall of Leela's house: samples of exotic items and rare objects brought back by her father from his epic travels – Nether wart, chorus fruit and dragon's breath to name just a few. To be such an expert potion brewer, her father must know so much about the different biomes in the world: their diverse flora and fauna; the mysterious, hidden dimensions.

"How does your dad know about all this stuff?" asks Cam. "He must read a lot of books."

"My dad always says that science isn't what's in books. It's what's out there in the world," replies Leela. "He says it's all about scientific enquiry."

She points to a diagram on the wall.

Types of Scientific Enquiry

Observing changes over time

Grouping and classifying

Research using secondary sources

Carrying out comparative and fair tests

Identifying patterns and trends

Asking questions

"If your dad believes that science is out in the world, why doesn't he let you go beyond the forest?" challenges Cam.

Leela picks up the note left by her dad. "Well, there's not much he can do about it right now, is there?"

Leela opens the large chest in the corner of the room, pulling out a wooden axe.

"Time for some scientific enquiry of our own!"

LIFE CYCLES: DEEP IN THE MANGROVES

A TROPICAL TREK

Our intrepid explorers set off excitedly, heading far past the forest boundary. The temperate trees slowly give way to dense, tropical jungle. They swing their wooden axes, hacking through the thick bushes in search of exotic flora and fauna to classify and categorise. As they yank aside a huge jungle vine, Cam suddenly finds his foot engulfed by sticky, oozing mud. The air is thick with the scent of salt and vegetation: they are in a mangrove swamp!

MANGLED MANGROVES

The unmistakable mangrove trees stand gnarled and tangled, creating a maze of waterways and channels. Leela has read about mangrove swamps: although they look dingy and dank, their elaborate root system creates the perfect home for a rich and diverse variety of life – perfect for our wannabe naturalists.

SIGNS OF LIFE

As they make their way through the swampy labyrinth, their eyes are drawn to a mass of translucent blobs floating in the water ahead of them…

"Bingo!" whispers Leela, pointing at the jelly-like orbs in the reeds.

LIFE CYCLES

Life cycle – the stages of development that an organism goes through from birth to death. This typically involves stages of birth, growth and reproduction.

At the heart of every life cycle is the process of **reproduction**, where new life is created and the cycle begins anew. Whether it be through the simple cell division of a single-celled organism or the elaborate courtship rituals of a mating pair, the drive to procreate is one of the most powerful forces in the natural world.

While the methods may differ from species to species, the end result is always the same: the creation of new life and the continuation of the cycle.

"What are those blobs in the water?" Cam queries.

Leela smiles excitedly. "Frogspawn!"

LIFE CYCLE OF AN AMPHIBIAN

Amphibians have a fascinating life cycle as, like insects, they go through a process called **metamorphosis**.

Metamorphosis – a biological process whereby the organism goes through significant changes in different stages.

Amphibians lay their eggs (spawn) in water. With frogs, for example, this frogspawn soon hatches into tadpoles, which are fully aquatic (can't leave the water) and breathe using their gills.

Tadpoles undergo a miraculous metamorphosis and grow legs, transforming into juvenile frogs. They eventually lose their tails and become adult frogs, now capable of spending time on land and breathing through newly formed lungs. In water, they can even breathe through their skin!

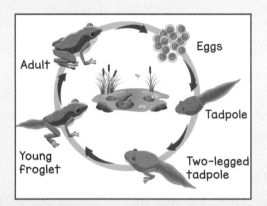

1

Metamorphosis in amphibians is a dramatic transformation.

Complete the sentences below.

Tadpoles breathe underwater using their .... When they

grow up and become frogs, they breathe through their ....

on land and through their .... in water.

2

Can you think of any other organisms that go through metamorphosis?

Circle **two** in the list below.

butterfly   tiger   parrot   bear   ladybird

Leela and Cam decide to build a small wooden hut for shelter while they observe the frogspawn. As they go exploring in search of wood, they cross a beach and spot the outline of a green turtle darting off into the ocean.

LIFE CYCLE OF A REPTILE

Reptile mothers lay their eggs on land (unlike amphibians, which lay their eggs in the water).

When the eggs hatch, a hatchling emerges and must avoid predators in order to survive this challenging stage of life. These hatchlings grow to become juveniles, before developing into full-grown adults capable of reproducing themselves.

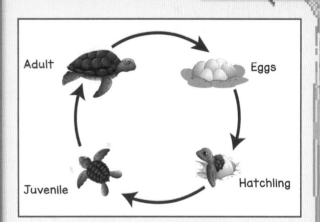

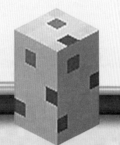

3

Give **two** differences between the life cycles of amphibians and reptiles.

....

....

....

....

While Cam builds the mangrove swamp hut, Leela checks her map and notices a bamboo jungle is close by. Maybe she'll fulfil her wish of spotting her favourite rare mammal...

LIFE CYCLE OF A MAMMAL

Mammals (including humans) give birth to live young and their mothers feed them milk. The baby grows inside its mother until it is ready to be born, then goes through a newborn stage when it relies on its mother to stay alive. Following this, it has a period of being an infant, like a cub or puppy (or toddler!), during which it is looked after by its mother. The mammal then enters the juvenile phase where it starts to become more independent and fend for itself.

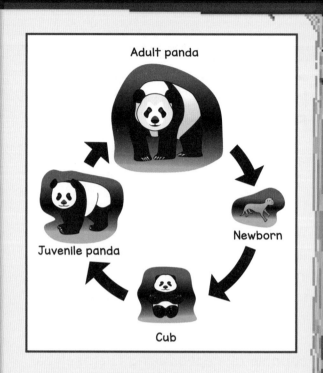

4

Let's record the features of the life cycles of different types of animal.

Complete the table below.

	Mammals	Reptiles	Amphibians
Give birth to live young			
Feed their young milk			
Lay their eggs in water			
Lay their eggs on land		✔	
Metamorphose			✔

5

Giant pandas are having a hard time finding potential partners to mate with. This is partly due to the destruction of their habitat.

Do you think humans **should** or **should not** interfere with endangered species to help them reproduce? What is your opinion?

....

....

....

....

....

....

....

....

....

....

....

PROJECT BUILDS

FROGGY FIELDWORK

It's now up to you to play the part of a budding naturalist and carry out some important fieldwork in the mangroves of Minecraft.

The warm frog variant spawns naturally in the mangrove swamps of the Overworld. It's your job to observe the entire life cycle of this charming creature and witness its dramatic metamorphosis from spawn to tadpole to a land-dwelling adult! And then you can observe it all over again and again. You'll just need a few slimeballs in your inventory.

In real life, frogs don't often live in mangroves because the saltwater dries them up. But, there is actually one species that does: the crab-eating frog (Fejervarya cancrivora). The famous naturalist, Charles Darwin, described it as "the frog that haunts the seaside". What an awesome adaptation!

Fieldwork is an important part of scientific research. Scientists **observe** the behaviour of an animal in its natural habitat and gather data about how it interacts with the world around it. This helps them to understand how animals adapt to different environments, and how they can be affected by changes to their habitat.

Creative

PROJECT 1:
OBSERVE THE FROG LIFE CYCLE

 `/locate biome mangrove_swamp`

1 Teleport to the mangrove swamp and try to spot a warm frog amongst the dense mangrove trees.

2 If you find two frogs, you can help them to breed by giving them slimeballs ⬤ *(Please note: frogs in real life **do not eat slimeballs**… it's just a Minecraft thing).* You will see hearts above their heads, which means they are ready to mate.

3 Once they have mated, one adult will waddle to the water to lay its frogspawn.

4 After about 10 minutes, some of the eggs will hatch into tadpoles.

5 The tadpoles will eventually become juvenile frogs. *(You can help speed up the process by giving them slimeballs but, again, this doesn't happen in real life.)*

6 Finally, you can help the newly adult frogs mate and watch the whole life cycle unfold again.

Creative

PROJECT 2: BUILD A TURTLE BEACH HUT

  /locate biome beach

You might think a turtle beach hut sounds blissful, but it's no time to relax: you have some important fieldwork to do! Zombies and their variants will trample on turtle eggs if they're out in the open. By gathering some important data, you can come up with ways to protect their nests from these menacing mobs.

Minecraft turtles breed when you give them seagrass. They lay their eggs on sand and an egg hatches in 4–5 Minecraft nights (and usually at night). So be prepared to lose some sleep to see the magic happen!

Creative

PROJECT 3: BUILD A PANDA BREEDING STATION

Pandas in Minecraft can be found in jungle and bamboo jungle biomes – and they are rare, just like in real life. So helping them reproduce can never be a bad thing! These cuddly mammals can be fed bamboo to encourage them to mate.

OVER TO YOU...

Roleplay Junior Geneticist

Minecraft pandas have different personality traits, such as lazy, worried, playful and aggressive. But get this: when two pandas breed, each one passes one of their traits to their offspring! When you breed pandas, try to identify which traits are passed on to their young.

CHAPTER ROUND-UP

FIELDWORK FULFILLED

Leela and Cam stand by the edge of the mangrove waters, watching the tadpoles swim away through the twisted tree roots. It is a magical moment and they know they have witnessed something rare and special – something seen only by fearless and adventurous scientists. As the sun begins to set, casting a warm orange glow across the swamp, they both feel a familiar sense of wonder at the natural world – and the endlessly repeating and miraculous cycles of life.

PROJECT NOTEBOOK

Use this space to reflect on your project builds.

• Did you observe the warm frog's life cycle?

• Do you have any ideas about how to protect turtle eggs on the nesting beaches?

• Did you notice any pandas pass on their personality traits to their young?

PLANTS: FROZEN FRONTIER

ICY EXPEDITION

The wind howls, whipping up plumes of snow that sting the faces of our two adventurers. Cam and Leela, pickaxes in hand, now find themselves battling through the icy tundra, ever further from home. Cam hopes to catch a glimpse of the majestic polar bear, whilst Leela seeks samples of plants that survive in the icy conditions.

EYE OF THE SNOWSTORM

As they slog their way across the snowdrifts, the sky and ground appear to merge into one disorienting swirl, like the centre of a snow globe. Leela clutches the compass in her hand: their only anchor to the world.

PERFECT BUILD SPOT

As they trudge on, the wind begins to die down and the snowfall subsides to a gentle flurry.

In the distance, they can see the perfect spot for their research hut, which will be a beacon of scientific discovery amidst a cold and hostile environment. With renewed hope and energy, Leela and Cam set their sights on the prime location, eager to build their base and begin their search for elusive wildlife.

"Here will be perfect," Cam declares, sticking his pickaxe into the snow to mark the spot for their research station.

"Perfect." Leela assesses their surroundings. "Now where shall we grow our food?"

Cam gawps at the frozen ground, stretching for miles...

THE PLANT LIFE CYCLE

Plants are fascinating living things that play an essential role in the vast web of life. From the delicate dandelion to the towering oak tree, these complex and adaptable organisms provide food for animals, create habitats for an array of life and even produce oxygen for organisms to breathe.

The wide range of plants in existence can be categorised into:
- non-flowering plants
- flowering plants, which can rely on bees, butterflies and other pollinators to **reproduce**.

Plants have adapted clever ways to survive in their environment, as well as innovative methods of spreading their seeds to continue their legacy on Earth.

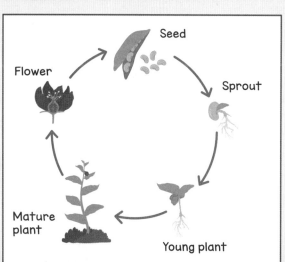

"You can't grow food here!" Cam declares.

"We can," asserts Leela confidently. "We'll just need to build a greenhouse next to the research station."

Cam laughs. "But for that we'd need–"

"These?" asks Leela, holding open her hand to reveal a variety of seeds.

"Mmm. Seeds." Cam pulls a sarcastic face. "My favourite..."

SEED GERMINATION

With flowering plants, it all starts with a seed. The seed contains an embryo and food stores: everything it will need to eventually begin its life as a plant. The seed is dormant, so it is alive, but it won't sprout (germinate) until perfect conditions are met.

The seed needs **water**, **oxygen** and **warmth** to germinate.

The seed case will absorb the water from the soil and eventually a shoot will break out and start growing above ground, stretching towards the sunlight.

Roots will grow downwards, making the plant stable and upright, as well as drawing up water from the soil.

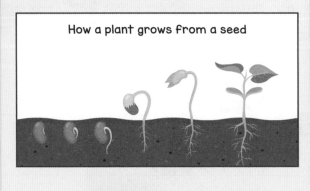

How a plant grows from a seed

1

a) Circle the **three** things in the list below that a seed needs to germinate.

water   carbon dioxide   oxygen   warmth   food   insects

b) Describe a challenge that seeds face in an extremely cold environment.

....

....

....

WHAT PLANTS NEED TO GROW

Like animals and humans, plants need particular things to survive and grow into adulthood.

- **Light:** plants need energy from the sun (or artificial light).
- **Air:** plants take in carbon dioxide through their leaves.
- **Water:** plants take in water through their roots.
- **Nutrients (in the soil):** plants need nutrients to support growth.
- **Space to grow:** plants need space for their root system and leaves to grow.

Plants make their own food through a process called **photosynthesis**. They take in carbon dioxide through their leaves and water through their roots. The leaves use the sun's energy to turn the carbon dioxide and water into glucose. Plants can then use that glucose as 'food'.

 2

Label the diagram with the **five** things plants need to grow. One has been done for you.

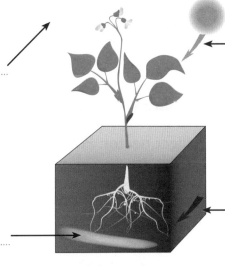

Space to grow

 3

What **three** things does a plant need to make its own food (by photosynthesis)?

As the low sun begins stretching shadows across the snow, Cam and Leela put the finishing touches on their research station. Taking a short break to enjoy the view, Leela's eye is drawn to a bright crimson poppy poking out of a patch of unfrozen grass.

PLANT REPRODUCTION

Flowering plants, like all living things, must find a way to successfully reproduce. Some plants achieve this by producing flowers that are brightly coloured with a sweet smell to attract pollinators, such as bees and butterflies.

Fertilisation – the coming together of the male and female pollens.

POLLINATION

Pollinators, such as bees, collect nectar from flowers as they move from one flower to another. During this movement, pollen from the male part of the plant (anther) attaches to the bee's body and then comes into contact with the female part (stigma) of the next flower, resulting in fertilisation and the creation of new seeds.

4

Put these statements in the correct order (from 1 to 5) to describe the pollination process.

The bee lands on the first flower to collect nectar. Pollen from the anther (male) gets stuck on its furry body.	
The flower of the plant will now fall away and the ovary will grow into a new seed (or fruit containing many seeds).	
The colourful petals and fragrant scent attract the bee to the first flower.	
Once the pollen has rubbed on the stigma of the second flower, it travels down the style and fertilises the ovary.	
The bee flies to the second flower to collect nectar and rubs the pollen from the first flower on the stigma (female) of the second flower.	

SEED DISPERSAL

Once the flower of the plant has been fertilised, it will become the **fruiting body**. This is where the new seeds will grow, ready to find somewhere to settle and eventually germinate when the conditions are right.

Have you ever blown a dandelion seed head into the air? Or have you noticed all the seeds in a tomato or watermelon? Tomatoes, watermelons and dandelion seeds are all examples of the **fruit** of the plant where the new seeds grow.

Remember that not all fruit is edible!

The seeds in these fruiting bodies need to find somewhere to grow, ideally far away.

Plants have adapted ingenious ways of spreading their seeds far and wide. Scientists call this **seed dispersal**.

 5

The table below categorises plants based on their method of **seed dispersal**.

Use the options given to complete the descriptions of the different dispersal methods.

explode   wind   water   animal

These seeds use the .... to travel to a new location. *Dandelion*	These seeds float on .... to find a new location. *Coconut*
These seeds stick to the fur of an .... to travel, or they grow inside delicious fruit which is eaten by the .... and passes through its digestive system. *Burdock* *Berries*	These seeds .... to spread to a new location. *Violet* *Peas*

PROJECT BUILDS

SUSTAINABLE GARDEN

It's now your turn to get your hands dirty and help Cam and Leela with their ice plains growing operation.

In Minecraft, you will build a greenhouse to grow food for their research station.

You should include some light sources, like glowstone or sea lanterns, so your water trenches don't freeze over.

You should also introduce bees as pollinators, which will help the growing operation run like a well-oiled machine.

Bees in Minecraft are very cute – and incredibly helpful! In their quest for delicious nectar from the attractive flowers, they pollinate your crops as they fly over them.

Of course, in real life, the bees would actually land on the flowers of your crop plants to pollinate them. Did you also know that real-life watermelon, potato, pumpkin and carrot plants all have flowers that are pollinated by bees? So next time you bite into a juicy watermelon, you know who to thank!

Pumpkin

Watermelon

Carrot

Potato

Creative

PROJECT 1: BUILD A GREENHOUSE

 /locate biome ice_plains

1 Teleport to an ice plains biome and find a good spot for your greenhouse with plenty of flat space (at least 16 × 16 blocks).

2 Use glass blocks to build your greenhouse. You could build a long, rectangular greenhouse (or a geodesic dome if you would like a challenge!).

3 Place dirt blocks on the ground. Your plants need soil to grow.

4 Dig trenches (which you will fill with water) between the rows of dirt. Plant the crops within 4 blocks of a water source to keep the soil hydrated.

5 Equip a water bucket and fill the trenches with water.

6 Now, use a hoe (use button) on the soil to prepare it for planting.

7 Plant seeds using the use/place button and wait for your crops to grow!

In real life, you would probably water your greenhouse crops with a hose or watering can. But in the world of Minecraft, it's enough to have irrigation channels filled with water that hydrate the soil. Just keep the water within 4 blocks of your growing crops!

Creative

PROJECT 2: BEE POLLINATION

The busy bees in Minecraft are attracted to flowers and other plants, including pink petals, cherry leaves and flowering azaleas. A bee collects pollen from a flower (you will see pollen spots on its abdomen) and it then drops pollen particles to fertilise plants below.

Minecraft bees can pollinate many crops, including carrot crops, pumpkin stems, beetroot crops and others. When one of these plants gets pollinated, it reaches the next growth stage (just as it would if you fertilised it yourself using bone meal).

Minecraft bees don't naturally spawn in the ice plains biome. However, in real life, the Arctic bumblebee (Bombus polaris) can survive and pollinate in colder climates, vibrating to increase its body temperature or warming itself inside the heat-reflective petals of the Arctic poppy!

1 Place a few beehives around your greenhouse.

2 Plant a range of brightly coloured flowers as a border around your vegetable patch. This will encourage the bees to circulate. Real-life bees love the common poppy!

3 Now introduce bees into your greenhouse. You can do this using a bee spawn egg.

4 Your bees will now travel between the beehives and the flowers, pollinating your crops as they pass. Thanks, bees!

OVER TO YOU...

Composters

Install a composter in your greenhouse. In real life, you can throw away old food and other organic materials onto a compost heap, and invertebrates process them into nutrients for the soil. In Minecraft, you can throw biological materials (e.g. food) into your composter and eventually collect bone meal, which you can use to manually speed up the growth of your crops.

CHAPTER ROUND-UP

DINNER IS SOLVED

Cam and Leela stand back to admire their masterwork in the midst of the ice plains. The greenhouse glistens in the bright sunlight, whilst busy bees buzz around inside, hovering between the carefully planted crops and perfectly placed flowers.

Together, Leela and Cam have transformed this frozen land into a thriving oasis, where crops can flourish and food will be plentiful. Through the glass of their immaculate structure, Cam thinks he sees a flash of white fur. He turns to Leela excitedly. "No way! Is that what I think it is?"

PROJECT NOTEBOOK

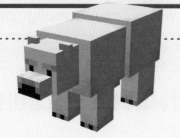

Use this space to reflect on your project builds.

- What was the result of your greenhouse project?
- What challenges did you face?
- How helpful were the bees in pollinating your crops?

ECOSYSTEMS: CORALS IN CRISIS

THE OVERWORLD OCEANS

The warm ocean: a biome full of wonders under the waves. Leela and Cam now find themselves swimming through the sunlit shallows of Rainbow Reef, gazing at technicolour shoals of tropical fish and sea turtles gliding through the vibrant coral. They both look at each other in amazement – they've never seen so many colours!

UNDERWATER ENCOUNTER

As Cam dives to examine a sea pickle, a dolphin suddenly appears, swimming playfully as if beckoning them to follow it. Our marine explorers look at each other excitedly: whilst they have come to observe the aquatic life that inhabits the reef, they've heard rumours that dolphins might lead a fortunate diver to the location of buried treasure.

TROUBLE IN THE REEF

As Leela and Cam follow the agile dolphin, they suddenly enter a large area of the coral that appears to have been destroyed. And where are all the fish and turtles?

"Looks like the work of underwater TNT," says Cam as he surfaces.

"There's a lot of tridents and rotten flesh floating around here," says Leela. "I'm guessing the locals used TNT to deal with a Drowned infestation."

She examines the damaged coral. "That's not gonna be good for the ecosystem."

ECOSYSTEMS

An **ecosystem** is like a big puzzle, where everything fits together perfectly.

Each piece is important and relies on the other pieces to survive. For example, in a savannah ecosystem, the grass feeds the antelopes, which in turn are food for the lions. And when the lions hunt, they help to control the population of antelopes, which allows the grass to grow.

But ecosystems are delicate and can be easily disrupted by things like pollution and deforestation.

Ecosystem – a community of living organisms (plants, animals and microorganisms) that interact with each other and their physical environment.

There are three main types of ecosystem: terrestrial (land), freshwater and marine (or ocean).

Leela and Cam observe the organisms in this marine ecosystem, marvelling at the myriad of species that call the reef their home.

1

Listed below are some ecosystems. Put them into the correct column of the table according to their type. Three have already been put into the table.

Forests   **Lakes**   **Grasslands**   **Tundra**   **Seagrass meadows**

Ponds   **Oceans**   **Rivers**   **Coral reefs**

Terrestrial ecosystems	Freshwater ecosystems	Marine ecosystems
Taiga	Wetlands	Coastal areas

2

Ecosystems are composed of things that are:

- **biotic:** living things within an ecosystem (these include animals, plants and microorganisms like algae and bacteria).

- **abiotic:** non-living things within an ecosystem (these include air, water, soil and rocks).

Here is a pond ecosystem.

Circle **five** biotic elements in one colour and **three** abiotic elements in another colour.

FOOD CHAINS

The biotic elements in ecosystems exist in food chains.

Food chains show how energy is transferred from one organism to another.

Food chains include producers, consumers and decomposers. The arrows show the transfer of energy.

Producers – plants and microorganisms that use energy from the sun and convert it into food (by a process called photosynthesis).

Primary consumers – herbivores that eat the producers and energy is transferred to them.

Secondary consumers – carnivores or omnivores that eat primary consumers and energy is transferred to them.

Decomposers – organisms that break down dead plants or animals into the substances that plants need to grow; examples of decomposers are fungi, bacteria and insects like earthworms and beetles.

Food chains work in a delicate balance. Increases or decreases in the population of an organism affect the other organisms in the food chain.

 3

Look at this food chain and answer the questions that follow.

dandelions   *rabbits*   *foxes*

a) If the population of foxes decreases, what will happen to the rabbit population? Tick **up** or **down**.

Up ☐   Down ☐

b) If the rabbit population increases, what will happen to the dandelion population? Tick **up** or **down**.

Up ☐   Down ☐

Our motivated marine researchers start swimming to shore but they spot a baby turtle darting among the dense corals. Cam gently pulls some seagrass from the sea bed and swims over to try to feed the little reptile.

Coral gets its stunning colours from the algae (called zooxanthellae) that lives inside it. Algae (a microorganism) is a producer that lives inside the coral in a codependent relationship, which means they help each other out: the algae produces food, which it shares with the coral, and the coral shares nutrients with the algae and provides shelter. A perfect partnership!

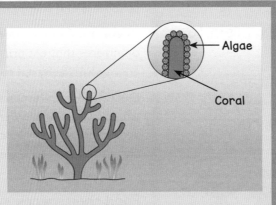

4

Look at the food chain below and answer the questions that follow.

algae   parrotfish   dolphin

If the algae population decreases, what will happen to the parrotfish population and the dolphin population?

a) Parrotfish population

Tick **up** or **down**.

Up ☐   Down ☐

b) Dolphin population

Tick **up** or **down**.

Up ☐   Down ☐

CORALS IN CRISIS

Coral reef ecosystems are vital because, despite only making up less than 1% of the oceans, they are home to 25% of marine creatures. These 'rainforests of the sea' can be damaged by human actions and their effects, such as pollution, overfishing and climate change.

Corals provide a habitat and shelter to many marine species. They also house algae, which is a key food source.

When coral becomes stressed from pollution or global warming, the algae leaves the coral, so that it looks bleached: grey and lifeless. But the coral, fish and turtles all need the algae to survive.

5

What do you think would be the impact on an ecosystem of a whole coral reef becoming bleached? Explain your thinking using the word bank below.

| algae | coral | primary consumers | secondary consumers |

COLOUR IN HOW MANY EMERALDS YOU EARNED

PROJECT BUILDS

RAINBOW REEF RESEARCH

Your job is to carry out some important research in Rainbow Reef. You will **build a dive centre** in Minecraft from which you can explore the rich and diverse coral reef ecosystem. You can also help gather data on turtle species, build a coral laboratory, and even create a turtle nursery to help protect baby turtles from the dastardly Drowned.

In real life, marine conservation charities do this kind of vital work (although they don't have to deal with any zombies). They restore coral reefs by helping corals reproduce in laboratories before transplanting them back onto the reef. They also monitor endangered turtle populations by tagging them with GPS tracking systems. Every part of the ecosystem is important, as they all exist in harmony with one another.

Marine conservation is the important work of protecting marine species and ecosystems in oceans and seas.

Creative

PROJECT 1:
BUILD A DIVE CENTRE

You should construct the dive centre close to the coral reef. This will be a base from which you can carry out important scientific work.

1 Create a coral laboratory

Design and build a coral laboratory from which you can role play as a coral scientist. Did you know that tube, brain and fire coral are all types of coral in real life?

2 Assemble an artificial reef

Constructing an artificial reef will create more habitats for marine life. You could use stone or concrete to create a simple 3D frame and cover it in a variety of coral species (only coral *fans* stick to the sides of blocks).

3 Build a turtle nursery

Breed turtles (encouraging them with seagrass) and care for their eggs and hatchlings. Zombies stomp on turtle eggs (and can even jump over a 1-block gap to reach them) and attack baby turtles on land during the night. Can you provide shelter for the turtles until they are big enough to be released back into the ocean?

Creative

PROJECT 2: TURTLE TRACKING

Gather data about these amazing marine reptiles by tracking their movements.

1 Place an anvil on the ground.

2 Get a name tag.

3 Write a good turtle name on the tag (e.g. Tommy).

4 Now put your new name tag in your inventory.

5 Find a turtle and lure it with some delicious seagrass.

6 Place your name tag on your turtle.

7 You can now teleport to your turtle whenever you want to track its location. Type the command into the chat:

/tp @s @e[type=turtle,name=Tommy]

Write down the coordinates of your turtle's changing location to gather data about where it's been travelling.

OVER TO YOU...

Glass-bottomed Boat

Want a way to monitor the marine wildlife without getting your hair wet? Build a glass-bottomed boat over the reef to make sure this rich ecosystem is working exactly as it should.

CHAPTER ROUND-UP

REEF AT PEACE

As the sun begins to set, Cam and Leela relax on the beach, looking out over the peace of Rainbow Reef. They are tired but satisfied with what they have achieved here. Over the distant waves they see a splash. Is that one of their tagged turtles?

Time to check it out and add it to the logbook!

PROJECT NOTEBOOK

Use this space to reflect on your project builds.

• What are you most proud of?

• How did you protect the turtles?

• How do you think you've made a difference to the ecosystem of Rainbow Reef?

ROCKS: A VIEW TO THE PAST

UNDER THE DESERT SUN

Cam and Leela now find themselves traipsing across the blistering desert. Cacti punctuate the arid landscape; their juicy stems look almost appetising in such hot and dry conditions.

OASIS OF SYMMETRY

As they pass a camel treading languidly across the sand, Cam spots an odd structure jutting out of the horizon. As they head towards it, they see it's some kind of ancient pyramid, adorned with mysterious symbols and constructed with flawless symmetry.

ANCIENT MYSTERY

Leela can't hide her excitement: she's heard rumours of elaborate temples and monuments of mysterious origin found scattered across the Overworld. They both approach the majestic structure, feeling an indescribable energy coming from the perfect pyramid.

"I wonder if there'll be loot inside!" shouts Cam, rubbing his hands together with glee.

"I'm more interested in artefacts that might tell us about the kind of people who built this place," says Leela. "Such structural beauty carved from pieces of rock!"

THE ROCK CYCLE

Rocks are some of the most ancient occupants of our Earth. Incredibly, scientists have measured some of the oldest rocks as being 4 billion years old!

And in this time, rocks have undergone repeated and dramatic transformations, caused by different processes including weathering, erosion, and intense heat and pressure inside the Earth's crust. Over these vast spans of time, rocks cycle through the different types, changing state and form. These recurring rock revolutions are called **the rock cycle**.

TYPES OF ROCK

Igneous rocks are formed from the cooling of molten rock (magma or lava).

Sedimentary rocks are formed by small rock pieces being transported in rivers and laid down in layers in the ocean.

Metamorphic rocks are formed from the other types of rocks that have undergone intense heat and pressure.

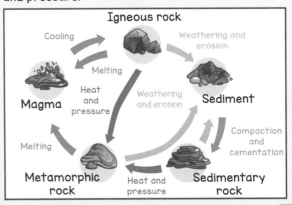

Igneous rock

Cooling

Weathering and erosion

Melting

Magma

Heat and pressure

Weathering and erosion

Sediment

Melting

Compaction and cementation

Metamorphic rock

Heat and pressure

Sedimentary rock

"Look, there are inscriptions on the blocks," Leela points out.

"Is the pyramid made of sand?" Cam asks.

"Sand?" chuckles Leela. "Sand would just fall down. No, it's built from sandstone."

SEDIMENTARY ROCKS

Rocks exposed on the Earth's surface undergo weathering and erosion.

Weathering refers to the breaking down of rocks on the Earth's surface. **Erosion** involves the breakdown of rocks by natural elements such as wind, ice or water, which then **transport** the debris into rivers, from where it accumulates in sediment layers on the ocean floor or within lakes and lagoons. Over time, these layers of sediment are compressed and compacted, forming sedimentary rocks like sandstone and limestone.

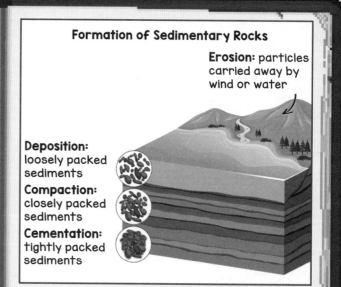

Formation of Sedimentary Rocks

Erosion: particles carried away by wind or water

Deposition: loosely packed sediments

Compaction: closely packed sediments

Cementation: tightly packed sediments

 1

Here is a picture showing layers of sedimentary rock.

Is the top or bottom layer the oldest? Explain your thinking.

....

....

....

 2

How do pieces of rock from the surface of the Earth end up at the bottom of the ocean?

....

....

Leela spots some suspicious sand and pulls out her brush to see if she can unearth any archaeological treasures. As Cam digs deeper in search of valuable loot, he breaks a sandstone block and hot lava comes pouring through the gap.

"Quick, hand me a water bucket!" cries Leela. She slings it onto the source of the lava flow, which turns into a solid, black block with gleaming purple flecks.

Leela's eyes light up. "Obsidian!"

IGNEOUS ROCKS

Igneous rocks are formed when magma, or lava, cools and solidifies. Magma is rock that is so hot, it has become a liquid!

Intrusive igneous rocks are formed when magma cools slowly in the Earth's crust. Examples include granite and diorite.

Extrusive igneous rocks are formed when magma comes out of the Earth (in the form of lava) and cools quickly, forming rocks like basalt and andesite.

Andesite   Basalt   Obsidian

Extrusive igneous rocks that have cooled quickly form small crystals, whereas intrusive igneous rocks that have cooled slowly form larger crystals. Rapidly cooling lava produces volcanic glass with no crystals (called obsidian).

 3

The size of crystals in igneous rocks is affected by the rate of magma or lava cooling.

Slow cooling forms larger crystals. Fast cooling forms smaller crystals (or no crystals).

Label the igneous rocks **intrusive** or **extrusive** based on their crystal size.

As Leela examines the mesmerising obsidian, Cam keeps digging and stumbles across four loot chests facing each other. Excitedly, he sprints towards them, but suddenly hears a clunking sound.

"Uh oh...pressure plate..." warns Cam. They both dive behind a wall just as the TNT explodes. When the dust clears, they see the blast has exposed a vast dripstone cave system. The walls are lined with dazzling deepslate.

METAMORPHIC ROCK

Metamorphic comes from the Latin words for 'changed form'. Metamorphic rocks are formed when igneous or sedimentary rocks are pushed down inside the Earth over time, and undergo intense heat and pressure, causing the form and structure of the rock to change. Examples include slate, marble and gneiss.

Slate   Marble   Gneiss

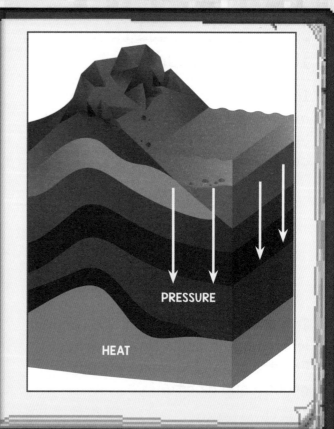

PRESSURE

HEAT

4

Explain why metamorphic rocks wouldn't exist without igneous or sedimentary rocks.

....

....

5

Why do you think metamorphic rocks form low down in the Earth's crust?

....

....

6

Look at the diagram below.

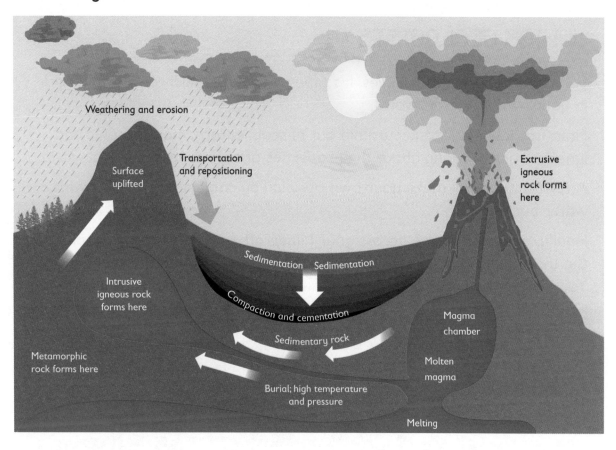

Why do you think it's called the rock **cycle**?

....

....

....

....

....

....

....

COLOUR IN HOW MANY
EMERALDS YOU EARNED

PROJECT BUILDS

JUNIOR GEOLOGISTS

So, you rookie rock detectives, it's time to explore the three types of rock in your own Minecraft world.

First, you'll build a stone pyramid out of sedimentary, metamorphic and igneous rock, thinking about the properties of each type in the real world.

After this, you will make your own obsidian by cooling lava rapidly with a water bucket.

Finally, you can venture across your Minecraft world collecting samples of the three types of rock that appear both in Minecraft and the real world. You're going to have to dig deep to find the courage to collect them all!

In real life, ancient civilisations like the Egyptians used sedimentary rock (such as limestone or sandstone) for building their famous pyramids.

They used igneous rock (such as granite, diorite and andesite) for their burial chambers or to line the passageways, as the crystals create a beautiful texture.

The ancient Maya used obsidian to make jewellery and weapons, as well as polishing it into a mirror which they believed let them see into the future!

Creative

PROJECT 1: BUILD YOUR OWN ROCK PYRAMID

To pay your respects to the ancient people, build your own stone pyramid in the desert. You must build it using the three types of rock.

1 Teleport to a desert biome.

2 Build a 20 × 20 frame. The example shown uses red sandstone to make it stand out.

3 Place a block inside one of the corners of your frame. Then place a block on top of this one, with another one coming off it (still inside your frame).

4 Now you can build the next layer of your pyramid (1 block in from the frame).

5 Then do the same thing again for the third layer.

6 Repeat the process until you reach the top of your pyramid!

PROJECT 2: MAKE YOUR OWN OBSIDIAN

Pour a water bucket on a lava source block to cool the lava rapidly. A 'source block' is the starting point of a flow of lava (or water).

Rapid cooling creates obsidian (volcanic glass).

In real life, cooling lava becomes extrusive igneous rock like obsidian, andesite or basalt. In Minecraft, when you cool lava with water, it becomes obsidian, stone or cobblestone. Cobblestone is large, round pebbles, called 'cobbles', bound together to make a rock-like paving material.

OVER TO YOU...

Display the Three Types of Rock

Use item frames to display samples of the three types of rock that are also found in Minecraft – you can use signs to label them. If you want a real challenge, you could go on this rock hunt in Survival mode! But getting your hands on basalt might require a trip to the Nether...

Visit the Badlands

The badlands biome is an impressive example of how land is formed from layers of rock, with its flat-mountain mesas and towering hoodoos carved out by erosion. In Minecraft they are made from terracotta, but in real life the badlands are formed from sedimentary rock (sandstone, limestone and mudstone).

Dig Down for Deepslate

In Minecraft, deepslate is found deep inside the crust of the world, much like the metamorphic rock slate in real life. Dig down and try to find some of this super-strong stone that's created by intense heat and pressure.

CHAPTER ROUND-UP

PUTTING THE LAST BLOCKS IN PLACE

Our fledgling stonemasons place the final block on a stone pyramid of their own, feeling a deep sense of respect for the ingenuity and craftsmanship of the mysterious builders of the desert temple. Leela decided to build a granite chamber inside, where she has stored a few personal items in a chest that would give a clue to the next visitor about who built this grand monument. Cam has constructed a secret room underneath the pyramid, lined with deepslate. He placed a single sign in the middle of the floor:

> Cam & Leela
> Woz
> 'Ere

PROJECT NOTEBOOK

Use this space to reflect on your projects.

• Can you remember what type of rock is formed from rapidly cooling lava?

• Did you find the three types of rock? Where did you find them?

• What materials did you use for your ancient temple?

RENEWABLE ENERGY: FOSSIL FUELS FIASCO

AS NIGHT FALLS

Our weary wanderers now find themselves navigating through a taiga forest before nightfall. Leela and Cam quickly debate where to build a shelter to get some sleep. But just as they agree upon a location, Leela spots the warm glow of a settlement beyond the treeline.

SMALL TOWN LIFE

A rickety bridge over a small stream marks the entrance to the little town. There is a relaxed buzz about the place: the citizens stand under lanterns, chatting to each other about the daily workings of small town life. A group of them gather by the well, the coal torchlight flickering on their faces.

A DARK PATH

Cam asks if there might be somewhere to stay for the night, and a woman gestures to an area that lies in complete darkness: not a torch or lantern to be seen. After a brief hesitation, they start down the dark path, but almost immediately Leela trips on a piece of wood. As she goes to put it back in place, she sees it is a sign marking an entrance, and she squints to make out the words scratched into the wood:

COAL MINE
CLOSED

"I think I can guess why this part of town is pitch black," says Leela.

ENERGY

Scientific and technological innovation by humans has produced many marvellous tools and systems to improve and enhance our lives.

Electricity, the motor vehicle and computerised systems are all examples of technology that have changed the world forever.

But all of these things, and many others, require power to run. And whilst humans have found ways of generating energy for these advanced aspects of our lives,

scientists have discovered that this has come with some negative side effects to the Earth we inhabit.

"We should help this side of town get their power back," says Cam, rifling through his bag and producing a few pieces of coal.

"Hmmm," utters Leela. "I've got a feeling that might run out."

NON-RENEWABLE ENERGY

Currently, the world relies heavily on fossil fuels as a source of energy. In fact, fossil fuels provide about 80% of the world's energy. These include coal, oil and natural gas. But these resources are non-renewable, meaning they will run out one day, and they are also harmful to the environment.

FOSSIL FUELS

Decomposing plants and other organisms that have become buried under layers of sediment and rock become useful energy sources, such as coal and oil. These form beneath the Earth's surface over millions of years before being mined and extracted. Coal, oil and gas are used for things like electricity, heating and transport.

But these finite resources will run out (as they take so long to form). In fact, scientists predict that oil, coal and natural gas will run out within the next 100 years.

 1

Approximately what percentage of the world's energy is currently provided by fossil fuels?

.... %

 2

What are the three fossil fuels that scientists predict will run out in the next 100 years?

Label the pictures below.

CLIMATE CHANGE

The use of fossil fuels is one of the greatest causes of climate change on our planet. The burning of these fuels releases what scientists call 'greenhouse gases' into the Earth's atmosphere, including carbon dioxide (CO_2). This creates a layer of gas around our planet that allows the sun's rays to enter, but traps the heat inside our atmosphere. Just like a garden greenhouse, this causes our environment to warm up.

Even small changes in the global temperature can have devastating effects, including rising sea levels, ecosystem damage and extreme weather events like wildfires, floods and hurricanes.

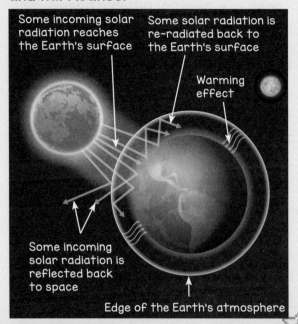

Some incoming solar radiation reaches the Earth's surface

Some solar radiation is re-radiated back to the Earth's surface

Warming effect

Some incoming solar radiation is reflected back to space

Edge of the Earth's atmosphere

3

Currently, about 44% of total carbon dioxide emissions come from coal.

Coal supplies $\frac{1}{3}$ of energy worldwide.

Which pie chart shows $\frac{1}{3}$? Tick the correct answer.

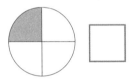   

4

What could happen to our planet if we continue to heavily use fossil fuels to create energy? Tick the correct answer.

Fossil fuels run out within the next **100** years ☐

The global temperature increases ☐

Sea levels rise ☐

Ecosystem damage ☐

Extreme weather events ☐

All of these ☐

RENEWABLE SOURCES

There are several alternative methods of generating energy that are renewable sources, which means they won't run out. In addition, they do not release greenhouse gases into the atmosphere.

These methods include solar energy, wind energy and hydro energy, which harness the naturally occurring power of the Earth.

There are other types of renewable energy, like geothermal and biofuel, but we will focus on solar, wind and hydro.

Solar energy
Uses the energy from the sun to generate power.

Wind energy
Uses the energy of the wind to generate power.

Hydro energy
Uses the energy of flowing water to generate power.

5

Complete the sentences in the table below using the given options.

solar　　wind　　water　　sun　　hydro　　wind

These are .... turbines. The .... blows the blades around in a circular motion, which generates energy.	This is a .... -electric dam. The .... flows through the dam at great pressure, which generates energy.	These are .... panels. The ....'s rays shine on their surface, which generates energy.

Cam and Leela find themselves a cold, empty house in the dark part of town, with a single lantern providing minimal heat. Unable to sleep, Leela begins imagining possible solutions to the village's power problems, only to be snapped out of it by Cam's loud snoring. (If only she could harness the energy of *that* raw power...)

6

Let's look at the **pros** and **cons** of non-renewable energy and renewable energy.

Look at the table below.

Non-renewable energy	Renewable energy
Could run out within the next 100 years	Won't run out
Harmful to the environment	Not harmful to the environment
Reliable	Expensive to set up
	Relies heavily on the weather, especially sunshine or wind

Do you think the world should switch to only renewable energy sources?

Explain your answer.

....

....

....

....

....

....

....

....

COLOUR IN HOW MANY EMERALDS YOU EARNED

PROJECT BUILDS

ECO-FRIENDLY ENERGY

Now, eco-warrior, Minecraft may not have real electricity or hydroelectric power... but it does have redstone!

You are going to simulate a working hydroelectric dam for the village. You will use redstone and sticky pistons to make a dam that lights a lamp when the water is flowing, and turns off the lamp when the water stops.

It's time to replace all of the non-renewable coal torches and lanterns with redstone lamps – and keep those dark-dwelling mobs at bay!

Can you help our eco-electricians connect the whole village on one big circuit?

Redstone is a made-up material that acts a bit like electricity. We will use it to behave like electricity but, just remember, redstone doesn't exist in real life. If only it did!

Creative

PROJECT 1: BUILD A HYDROELECTRIC DAM

  /locate structure village*

For Java edition, you must specify the type of village to locate, e.g. /locate structure village_plains

1 Teleport to a village.

2 Find a river or lake close to the village (or create your own).

3 Now build a wall (2 blocks thick) across your river or lake to act as a dam. The bottom of your wall should touch the river bed.

4 Break 2 or 3 holes vertically in the wall where your water will come out.

5 Equip a water bucket and place water in the holes to create flowing water sources.

6 Now, you should place sticky pistons 2 blocks above the water holes (sticky side facing down). Use blocks attached to the top of the wall so you have something to place the sticky piston on (you can remove them later).

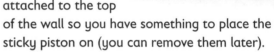

7 Next, place wooden planks under the sticky pistons, which will block the flowing water when they are activated.

8 Now, connect the sticky pistons to a single lever (using redstone dust if you need to).

9 Finally, you need to run redstone dust from the lever to a solid block and place a redstone torch on the opposite side of the block. Then run redstone dust from next to the redstone torch to your redstone lamp. This will invert the signal: which means when the lever is OFF, the lamp is ON. This is so the lamp comes on when the water is running!

Creative

PROJECT 2:
BUILD A LIGHTING SYSTEM FOR THE VILLAGE

1 From your redstone lamp, connect a redstone repeater pointing away from the lamp.

2 Now use redstone dust to connect your lamp to the closest house.

3 To increase the redstone signal, use redstone repeaters every 15 blocks.

4 In the house, install a redstone lamp and connect it to your redstone dust. Remember that redstone dust can't run vertically up surfaces, so you will have to build ramps using blocks.

5 You must connect the whole village to one redstone circuit, with the only redstone power source being your hydroelectric dam.

Can you help to keep the monsters out of the village using a single power source?

OVER TO YOU...

Test your Lighting System

Switch to Survival mode and increase the difficulty level to Easy, Normal or Hard. Set the time to Sunset and see if you've illuminated the village well enough to prevent mobs from spawning inside it. No-one wants to hop out of bed during the night and bump into a bow-wielding skeleton...

Sustainable Living

Using renewable energy in real life is sustainable, which means it can be used continuously without running out or damaging the environment. How else can you be sustainable in a Minecraft world? In Survival mode, if you chop down a lot of trees for wood, how could you make sure that you don't use up all the available forest?

CHAPTER ROUND-UP

A BRIGHTER FUTURE

Dusk is looming. Our inventive engineers have connected the last lamp to their redstone circuit, and now it is time to see if their hard work has paid off. Townsfolk gather round curiously, as Leela nods to Cam to activate the mechanism. With a hopeful look on his face, Cam yanks the lever. The network of lamps fires up, illuminating the settlement in a hazy glow of warmth and security.

Cam and Leela smile at each other, proud that their ingenious idea has been brought to life. They are sure the residents will sleep soundly tonight.

PROJECT NOTEBOOK

Use this space to reflect on your project builds.

• Did you manage to simulate a working dam?

• What was the most challenging part of the project?

• What did you learn about redstone for next time?

HABITAT AND ADAPTATION: AQUATIC ENIGMA

DARK FOREST

The adventurous pair now traipse through a dark forest, their eyes scanning for a flash of the characteristic pink flowers of an azalea tree. They know this rare tree's long roots mark the presence of a mysterious underground habitat: the lush caves. Cam nudges Leela and points ahead – the first stage of their search is over.

CAVE OF WONDERS

They locate the rooted dirt beneath the azalea tree and dig down, eventually reaching the cave below. The air is dense and humid, the walls adorned with thick moss and vines. Moist dewdrops fall from the dripleaves as our excited naturalists edge deeper and deeper into the cavern, past the spore blossoms and hanging glow berries.

A RARE SIGHTING

They both creep quietly, determined not to scare away the creature they have come in search of. They crouch and manoeuvre under a waterfall, the roaring water somehow helping with their laser focus. Just as they emerge from the rushing flow, they spot it. A single, rare salamander: the beloved axolotl!

Leela glares at Cam. The message is clear: don't make a sound. They've both been desperate for a sighting of this elusive animal, and Leela isn't going to have anyone mess with her chance of encountering one close up. She pulls a water bucket from her inventory and clutches it tightly, tiptoeing ever closer to the unsuspecting amphibian.

HABITAT AND ADAPTATION

Animals and plants have evolved fascinating adaptations, to help them survive and thrive in their unique and often challenging environments.

From the blazing heat of the desert, to the inhospitable cold of the tundra, these evolutionary agile organisms have adopted fascinating features that haven't appeared overnight.

In fact, these adaptations have developed over thousands or millions of years to help that species become better suited to the specific climate and features of the habitat they call their home.

"Got it!" exclaims Leela, as she scoops up the axolotl in her bucket.

"What do we do with it now?!" Cam asks, panicking.

"Study it, of course!" she announces. "You see, a lot can be learned through careful study of the axolotl's unique adaptations."

CAMEL ADAPTATIONS

Camels are a fantastic example of animal adaptation in action.

These robust and resilient mammals live in hot, dry deserts where water is scarce.

There are three species of camel: the one-humped dromedary (which makes up 94% of the world's camel population), the two-humped Bactrian camel and the endangered wild Bactrian camel.

Camels have adapted the following features over millions of years to survive in their hot desert habitats.

Hump to store fat | Long eyelashes | Nostrils that open and close

Can tolerate temperature changes in the body without needing to sweat

Can survive for over a week without water

Can drink up to 46 litres of water in one drinking session

Wide feet

 1

Draw lines to match each adaptation to how it helps camels survive in their desert habitat.

Adaptation	How it's suited to its habitat
Hump to store fat	Can last for long periods in dry conditions
Long eyelashes	Can walk on sand without sinking
Nostrils that open and close	Keeps sand out of the camel's nose
Can survive for over a week without water and can drink a lot in one go	Keeps sand out of the camel's eyes
Wide feet	They reduce water loss from sweating in the hot conditions
Tolerates changes in body temperature without sweating	The fat can be turned into energy

POLAR BEAR ADAPTATIONS

Polar bears offer us insight into animal adaptations from the other end of the climate spectrum. These tough, fearsome predators stalk the frozen tundra looking for their next meal, all the while being perfectly adapted to survive in the cold, unforgiving Arctic.

Their physical characteristics have changed over hundreds of thousands of years to enable them to be masters of their environment: moving over the ice, swimming in freezing cold water and preying on fatty seals.

Unfortunately, being perfectly adapted to the environment becomes challenging when that habitat is threatened owing to human actions (as is happening due to climate change).

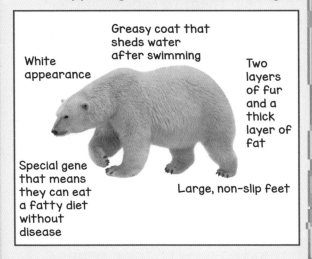

Greasy coat that sheds water after swimming

White appearance

Two layers of fur and a thick layer of fat

Special gene that means they can eat a fatty diet without disease

Large, non-slip feet

Complete the table to show how each adaptation helps polar bears survive in their Arctic habitat. One has been done for you.

Adaptation	How it's suited to its habitat
White appearance	Provides camouflage in the white snow and ice
Thick layers of fur and fat	
Greasy coat that sheds water after swimming	
Large, non-slip feet	
Special gene means they can eat a fatty diet	

AMAZING ADAPTATIONS

Animals, plants, insects and humans have all adapted unique features that help them to survive in their habitat. These adaptations help them to defend against predators, find food and water, or survive in extreme climates.

> Adaptations develop due to **natural selection**. This means that organisms which are better suited to their environment have a higher chance of surviving and passing on their genes.

Cacti are well adapted to survive in hot deserts because they have:

* stems that can store water
* a thick, waxy outer layer that helps to reduce water loss
* extensive root systems that can collect water from a large area or deep underground
* spines, rather than leaves, to reduce water loss and protect themselves from animals that might want to eat them.

3

Underneath each picture, write down one adaptation that the organism has developed and how you think it helps the organism survive, defend itself or find food.

Hedgehog	**Leaf insect**	**Owl moth**

....	....	....
....	....	....

Giraffe	**Tortoise**	**Hummingbird**

....	....	....
....	....	....

HUMAN ADAPTATIONS

Humans are arguably the best adapted species on our planet. People have adapted to live in a wide range of different habitats and have thrived in each of them. This is due to a number of key adaptations which have put humans ahead of other organisms.

Complex brain

The human brain is an incredible organ that helps people to plan, problem solve and communicate: all skills that have contributed to our great ability to survive.

Opposable thumbs

Having a thumb on the opposite side to the fingers has allowed humans to craft tools and weapons, make fire and do countless other useful things.

Sweating

It might not be the most charming physical feature, but sweating allows humans to cool down in hot conditions. Other animals have to pant to cool down, which they can't do whilst running. This gives humans a great advantage.

4

Listed below are some behavioural adaptations that humans have evolved over millions of years. Write how you think the adaptation has helped humans to survive.

a)   Making fire

....

....

b)   Throwing weapons

....

....

c)   Learning from others

....

....

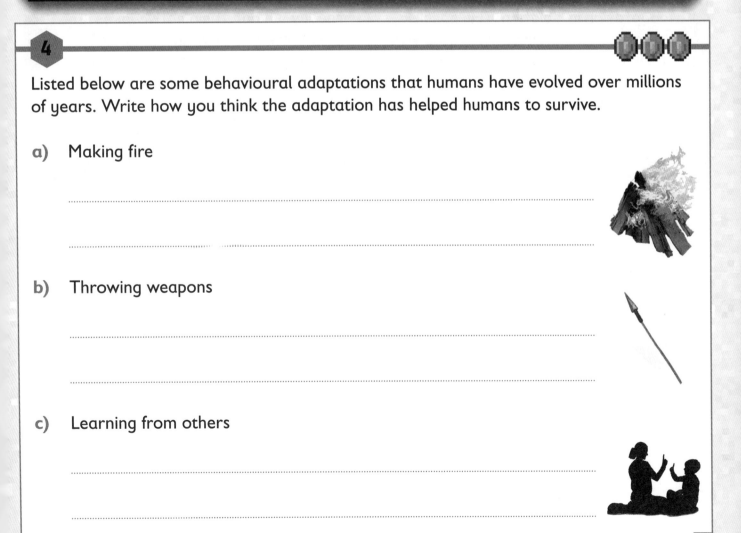

"Now we will build our own axolotl pond! Then we can conduct our important research." Leela announces excitedly. "We'll need to recreate its unique lush caves habitat, so before we go, we need..."

"Cave vines, spore blossoms and dripleaves," interrupts Cam.

Leela looks at him, impressed.

AXOLOTL ADAPTATIONS

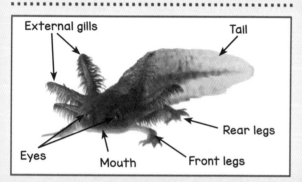

External gills

Tail

Eyes

Mouth

Front legs

Rear legs

The axolotl is a stunning example of adaptation in isolation. This specific species of salamander only lives wild in two lakes in Mexico – and one of its most intriguing adaptations is to do with its life cycle.

Forever young

Salamanders are amphibians, which means they usually go through **metamorphosis** (see page 10). However, unusually, axolotls don't go through metamorphosis. So, they keep their feathery gills and their larval tail (used for swimming) and continue to live in the water.

Scientists don't know exactly why this adaptation developed. One theory is that their native lakes never dry up (like many bodies of water), so they never had to develop body parts for surviving on land.

5

This diagram shows the life cycle of an axolotl.

How is the life cycle of an axolotl different to that of a frog?

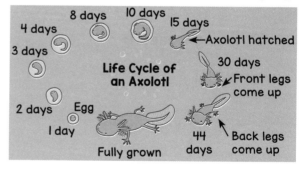

Life Cycle of an Axolotl

3 days
4 days
8 days
10 days
15 days
←Axolotl hatched
2 days
Egg
1 day
30 days
Front legs come up
44 days
Back legs come up
Fully grown

....

....

....

....

MEDICAL MARVEL

The other major adaptation that has occurred in the axolotl population is their miraculous ability to regrow limbs, organs and even their brain! If they are wounded, the injured part simply grows back as a copy of the original.

This ability to regrow lost body parts is a huge reason why these unique salamanders are studied for medical research. Scientists hope that they can use the scientific knowledge to one day help cure disease and heal injuries in humans.

Endangered in the wild

Unfortunately, wild axolotl populations are critically endangered due to urban development, habitat loss, pollution and non-native species being introduced into their lake habitat in Mexico. The graph below shows some data collected by scientists.

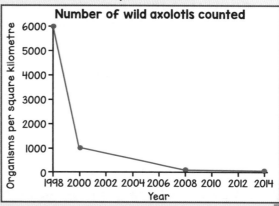

6

Look at the graph above for this question.

In 2014, scientists counted only 35 axolotls per square kilometre.

How many axolotls did they find in 1998 per square kilometre? ....

7

What do you think humans could do to help protect wild axolotls?

Write your ideas below.

....

....

....

....

PROJECT BUILDS

A HABITAT TO CALL HOME

Now, adaptation experts, axolotls also exist in the wonderful world of Minecraft and are **perfectly adapted** to their lush caves habitat. Whilst 'lush caves' isn't technically a real-world habitat, it does include many features that are similar to the axolotls' real-life lake habitat in Mexico. It has water, darkness and lots of hiding places!

Minecraft axolotls are aquatic mobs that can venture onto land, but only 8 or 9 blocks from the water – in fact, they can die after 6000 game ticks (5 minutes) of being out of water. How is this similar to real-life axolotls? The answer is that real axolotls mostly stay underwater, only coming onto land for short periods of time.

The other interesting feature of Minecraft axolotls is that if they take damage underwater, they play dead and then heal themselves with Regeneration. This mirrors their miraculous real-life ability to regrow limbs and other organs.

You are going to help Cam and Leela by catching a wild axolotl. You will also build your own axolotl pond: this should include all of the features of their natural lush caves habitat that they are perfectly adapted to, so they feel right at home! From this pond you can help breed axolotls to increase the wild population.

You might know that the probability of a blue axolotl spawning is 1 in 1200. What you might not know is that this number was chosen because there are approximately 1200 real-life axolotls left in the wild. So, let's give these little critters some love!

Creative

PROJECT 1: CATCH A WILD AXOLOTL (OR TWO!)

1 First, you need to find a lush cave as it's the only place you will find a wild axolotl. But there's a catch: the /locate command doesn't work for lush caves, so you are going to have to search for one by locating an azalea tree. Azalea trees can spawn on the surface in any biome. Look out for their distinct pink flowers and knotted roots.

When you find an azalea tree, dig down underneath it and you will eventually find a lush cave.

2 Find a wild axolotl – remember they are rare (and endangered in the real world) so they might not be easy to spot. Axolotls will only spawn underwater in lush cave pools where clay can be found 5 blocks or fewer beneath them.

3 Catch the wild axolotl in a water bucket.

4 Make a note of all the features of their lush cave habitat in a book and quill 📖. You will need to know all of the things that are found in a Minecraft axolotl habitat so you can later recreate their habitat in your axolotl pond.

5 Now travel above ground to find a good location for your new home for this fascinating amphibian.

Creative

PROJECT 2:
BUILD AN AXOLOTL POND

1 First, find the side of a hill (or a natural cave) so that later on you can hang some glow berries and other plants from overhanging blocks.

2 Next, replace the ground with the types of rock you identified in the axolotls' natural habitat. For example, if you found deepslate in the lush cave, use that in your new axolotl habitat. You want your axolotls to feel right at home!

3 Now dig a shallow hole in the ground for the pond. Make sure you have a slope going up to the ground, as axolotls do sometimes leave the water for short periods of time.

4 Fill your pond with water using a water bucket. Make sure you place water in every space around the edge of the pond so the water is still.

5 Decorate the inside and outside of your pond with all of the features of a lush cave – open your book and quill to check the list you made.

6 Add some overhanging blocks that stick out of the side of the hill or cave. You can hang some glow berries and spore blossoms (to create some shade).

7 Finally, you can breed your captive axolotls then reintroduce them into the lush caves to increase the wild population!

OVER TO YOU...

Breeding Axolotls

You can help them to breed by giving two axolotls a bucket of tropical fish. They will enter 'love mode' and reproduce (but please note, in real life axolotls lay eggs – sometimes up to 1000).

CHAPTER ROUND-UP

A BRIGHTER FUTURE

Leela and Cam watch the axolotls splashing around with great satisfaction. This has been a difficult but rewarding expedition! The long and arduous hunt for an azalea tree; the ceaseless search for a wild axolotl specimen. Then finally seeing the newly bred axolotls thriving in their new habitat.

Leela is excited to start studying these rare creatures. And despite the unlikely odds, Cam still holds out hope that the next one might be a super-rare blue axolotl.

But, they both agree that it will soon be time to head home to Avondale, as Leela's father should be returning.

PROJECT NOTEBOOK

Use this space to reflect on your project builds.

- Describe how you found a wild axolotl.
- How did you make sure your pond was perfectly suited to your axolotls?
- What are you most proud of about your conservation and research project?

ANSWERS

Pages 10–13

1. Missing words in this order are: gills; lungs; skin
   [1 emerald each]

2. butterfly; ladybird [1 emerald each]

3. Amphibians undergo metamorphosis, unlike reptiles.
   [1 emerald]
   Amphibians lay their eggs in water, whereas reptiles lay their eggs on land. [1 emerald]

4. The table should be completed as follows:
   Give birth to live young: **Mammals** ✔
   Feed their young milk: **Mammals** ✔
   Lay their eggs in water: **Amphibians** ✔ [1 emerald each]

5. Award yourself up to 3 emeralds using this guidance:
   For only stating your opinion (e.g. should or should not interfere). [1 emerald]
   For stating your opinion and providing a supporting reason (e.g. I think humans should help endangered species reproduce because…). [2 emeralds]
   For stating your opinion and providing more than one supporting reason, or providing a balanced argument (e.g. On one hand, I think we should help endangered species reproduce because…. However, it could be argued that humans shouldn't interfere because…). [3 emeralds]

Pages 20–23

1. a) water; oxygen; warmth [1 emerald each]
   b) Any suitable answer, e.g.
   Seeds need warmth to germinate.
   Seeds need water to germinate and water often turns to ice in very cold environments.
   Seeds need to embed themselves in soil, which could be frozen solid in a cold environment.
   [1 emerald]

2.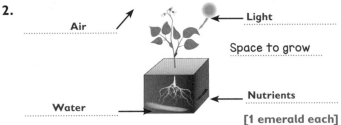

   Air

   Light

   Space to grow

   Nutrients

   Water
   [1 emerald each]

3. carbon dioxide; water; energy [1 emerald each]

4. The table should be completed from top to bottom with this numbering: 2, 5, 1, 4, 3 [1 emerald each]

5.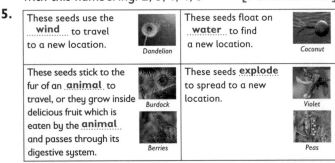

   These seeds use the **wind** to travel to a new location. *Dandelion*

   These seeds float on **water** to find a new location. *Coconut*

   These seeds stick to the fur of an **animal** to travel, or they grow inside delicious fruit which is eaten by the **animal** and passes through its digestive system. *Burdock* *Berries*

   These seeds **explode** to spread to a new location. *Violet* *Peas*
   [1 emerald each]

Pages 30–33

1. The table should be completed as follows:
   Terrestrial ecosystems: Forests; Grasslands; Tundra
   Freshwater ecosystems: Lakes; Ponds; Rivers
   Marine ecosystems: Seagrass meadows; Oceans; Coral reefs [1 emerald each]

2. **Biotic elements:** any living organisms can be circled, such as the ducks, snake, frog, fish, trees and plants.
   [1 emerald each up to a maximum of 5]
   Abiotic elements: any non-living features can be circled, such as air, water, soil and rocks.
   [1 emerald each up to a maximum of 3]

3. a) Up [1 emerald]
   b) Down [1 emerald]

4. a) Down [1 emerald]
   b) Down [1 emerald]

5. Award yourself up to 4 emeralds using this guidance:
   For using part of the word bank. [1 emerald]
   For using all of the word bank. [2 emeralds]
   For explaining how the bleaching of the coral reef would have knock-on effects for the rest of the ecosystem. For example, algae leaving the coral means less food for the primary consumers, which in turn means less food for the secondary consumers. [2 emeralds]

Pages 40–43

1. Award yourself up to 2 emeralds using this guidance:
   For stating the bottom layer is the oldest. [1 emerald]
   For explaining how you know this. For example, sediment is deposited at the bottom of the ocean in layers over time (so the bottom layer must be the oldest). [1 emerald]

2. They are eroded and then transported by rivers [1 emerald] before slowly sinking (settling) to the bottom of the ocean. [1 emerald]

3.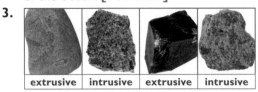

   | extrusive | intrusive | extrusive | intrusive |
   [1 emerald each]

4. Award yourself up to 2 emeralds using this guidance:
   For explaining how metamorphic rocks were once sedimentary and igneous rocks. [1 emerald]
   For mentioning that they are formed from sedimentary and igneous rocks under intense heat and pressure.
   [1 emerald]

5. Because of the intense heat and increased pressure low down in the Earth's crust. [1 emerald]

6. Award yourself up to 5 emeralds using this guidance:
   For explaining your thoughts and giving a valid reason. For example, I think it is called the rock cycle because the different rocks transform and change their structure continuously over time. [3 emeralds]

For adding information about the specific processes of transformation. For example, sedimentary rock that is pushed low down into the Earth's crust undergoes intense heat and pressure and transforms into metamorphic rock. **[2 emeralds]**

Pages 50–53

1. 80% **[1 emerald]**
2.

coal	gas	oil

[1 emerald each]

3.

[1 emerald]

4. All of these ✔ **[1 emerald]**
5.

These are ....wind.... turbines. The ....wind.... blows the blades around in a circular motion, which generates energy.	This is a ...hydro-electric dam. The ..water.... flows through the dam at great pressure, which generates energy.	These are ....solar.... panels. The ......sun.....'s rays shine on their surface, which generates energy.

[1 emerald each]

6. Award yourself up to 4 emeralds using this guidance:
   For stating your opinion. **[1 emerald]**
   For stating your opinion and providing one supporting reason. **[2 emeralds]**
   For stating your opinion and providing two supporting reasons. **[3 emeralds]**
   For stating your opinion and providing several supporting reasons and/or considering the pros and cons (a balanced argument). **[4 emeralds]**

Pages 60–63

1. Boxes joined as follows:

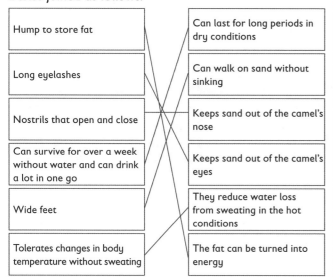

[1 emerald each]

2. Any suitable answers, e.g.

Adaptation	How it's suited to its habitat
White appearance	Provides camouflage in the white snow and ice
Thick layers of fur and fat	Keeps the polar bear warm in the ice-cold temperatures of the Arctic
Greasy coat that sheds water after swimming	Helps the polar bear to keep warm after leaving the water / Reduces the mass of its coat to make it more agile on the ice
Large, non-slip feet	Helps the polar bear to keep grip and move fast across the ice
Special gene means they can eat a fatty diet	Allows the polar bear to survive on a diet mainly of seal meat and fat

[1 emerald each]

3. Any suitable answers, e.g.
   Hedgehog: sharp spines protect it from predators **[1 emerald]**
   Leaf insect: camouflage helps disguise it from predators **[1 emerald]**
   Owl moth: the owl-like appearance of the wings helps to protect it from predators **[1 emerald]**
   Giraffe: Long neck enables it to feed from high branches **[1 emerald]**
   Tortoise: hard shell protects it from predators **[1 emerald]**
   Hummingbird: Long beak enables it to drink the nectar of flowers **[1 emerald]**
4. Any suitable answers, e.g.
   a) Has enabled humans to keep warm in cold conditions **[1 emerald]**
   b) Has enabled humans to hunt animals for food **[1 emerald]**
   c) Has enabled humans to develop their skills/intelligence **[1 emerald]**
5. Award yourself up to 2 emeralds using this guidance:
   For stating that axolotls don't undergo metamorphosis. **[1 emerald]**
   For mentioning specific details like axolotls keeping their gills and larval tail, or explaining that axolotls continue to live in the water. **[1 emerald]**
6. 6000 **[1 emerald]**
7. Any suitable answer, e.g.
   Humans could:
   create protected areas
   help axolotls breed in the wild
   reduce lake pollution
   reduce urban development and habitat loss
   raise awareness. **[1 emerald for each idea up to a maximum of 3]**

STORY ROUND-UP

HOME AGAIN

Our heroes return to Avondale and enter Leela's house, only to find her father looking up at them sternly from his potion stand. Leela quickly opens her bag and pulls out a variety of items she's collected from her journey: slimeballs; a heart of the sea; some golden apples.

"I brought these back for you," she quivers. "I thought you might have some use for them."

Leela's dad's serious face soon gives way to a hint of glowing pride.

"You're just like me when I was your age," he chuckles warmly. "Maybe you are ready for a bit more of an adventure."

SPEND YOUR EMERALDS!

Leela's father invites Leela and Cam on a trip to the hostile Nether to collect potion ingredients.

You've earned emeralds by answering questions throughout the adventure. Spend them in the shop below to equip our heroes with the best weapons and armour for their dangerous journey.

Can you afford a full set of diamond armour?

Tools					
stone	3	4	4	2	3
iron	4	5	5	3	4
gold	6	7	7	5	6
diamond	9	10	10	8	9

Armour				
iron	4	5	4	3
gold	5	6	5	4
chain	7	8	7	6
diamond	10	13	11	10